CHRISTIAN SEX EDUCATION FOR KIDS

8-12 YEAR OLDS

Discover What God Says About Sex,
Puberty, Relationship, Boundaries, and
Growing Up
(Puberty Book For Kids)

Sharon L. Taylor

Sharon L. Taylor

Sharon L. Taylor

TABLE OF CONTENT

Sharon L. Taylor

Introduction

Purpose of the Book:
Why This Book is Essential for Young Christians

Hello! I'm so glad you're here, diving into a book about God's wonderful design for us as His children. If you're holding this book, you're probably curious about some big questions— questions about our bodies, changes we go through, friendships, and the things that make us... well, us!

But if you've ever felt a little nervous or embarrassed to talk about these things, you're not alone. Many kids and even adults feel this way.

That's because conversations about our bodies and growing up haven't always been easy or common, even in Christian homes. But here's the good news: this book is here to make those conversations feel natural and safe.

So why did I write this book?

I wrote it because I believe that every young Christian deserves a space to learn about God's design for their body, emotions, and relationships in a way that's fun, honest, and true to His teachings.

God has wonderful plans for us, and learning about these plans helps us live in the best possible way He intended.

Understanding the Purpose of Sex Education in Christian Faith

Let's start by answering a big question: why do Christians even need sex education?

Can't we just talk about faith, kindness, and being good people?

Of course, we should focus on those things, but there's so much more to living as a child of God. God didn't just create us as spirits or minds; He gave us bodies, too.

And those bodies are designed to grow, change, and develop in unique ways. God gave us instructions on how to live in all areas of life, including how we care for and respect our bodies and relationships.

This book will be like a roadmap, guiding you through the changes you'll experience, showing you what the Bible says about growing up, and answering questions you might have but don't know how to ask.

I want to help you feel prepared, confident, and most importantly, loved by God in all aspects of who you are.

Understanding God's Design: How God Created Us as Unique Individuals

Now, let's talk about something exciting— you!

Did you know that you are one of a kind?

The Bible tells us in Psalm 139:14, "I praise you because I am fearfully and wonderfully made." Isn't that amazing?

God designed every part of you, from your head to your toes, and He did it with such love and care.

Just like no two snowflakes are the same, no two people are exactly alike. God gave you a special personality, unique gifts, and even the ability to grow and change.

As we go through this book, I want you to remember that everything about you is part of God's plan. Your body, your thoughts, your feelings—all of these things are known and loved by God.

And because God made you, you're not a mistake. You are exactly who you are meant to be. Knowing this can help you feel proud and confident as we talk about some things that might be new or even a little strange at first

Learning to See Ourselves
Through God's Eyes

Imagine for a moment that God is an artist and you are His masterpiece. Every brushstroke, every color, and every detail is chosen carefully. That's how much thought went into making you.

This idea helps us see that our bodies aren't just random; they have a purpose. As we learn about our bodies, our relationships, and what the Bible teaches about these things, we're not just learning facts.

We're discovering the beautiful, intricate ways God made each of us.

Through this book, I hope you'll feel excited to see yourself as God's creation, with all the unique things that make you.

We'll talk about how our bodies grow and change, but we'll also explore the amazing ways God gives us emotions, relationships, and a sense of belonging.

Each part of who we are points back to God's wonderful plan.

What the Bible Teaches About Our Bodies, Sexuality, and Boundaries

Now that we know a bit more about why this book is important and how special you are, let's look at what the Bible has to say about our bodies and sexuality.

I know that's a big word, and it might feel a little strange. But when we talk about sexuality here, we're talking about something God created as a part of who we are.

The Bible is full of wisdom on living in a way that honors God, and it has a lot to say about how we should think about our bodies and relationships.

In the book of Genesis, we see that God created the first humans, Adam and Eve, and He designed them to be in a loving relationship with each other.

God's design for relationships, especially the deep, special relationship of marriage, is based on love, respect, and trust.

But until that time comes (which is a long way off!), God gives us guidelines to help us live in a way that respects our own bodies and the boundaries of others.

What Boundaries Mean and Why They're Important

Have you ever played a game like soccer or basketball?

Every game has rules, right?

These rules aren't there to make the game less fun; they're there to make sure everyone plays safely and has a good time. Boundaries work the same way.

God gives us boundaries because He loves us and wants what's best for us. Boundaries are guidelines about how we interact with others, how we take care of our bodies, and how we respect the bodies and personal space of others.

The Bible teaches us about these boundaries, and as we go through this book, we'll explore what those boundaries look like in friendships, family relationships, and more.

We'll learn that respecting ourselves and others isn't just a rule; it's a way to show love and kindness, just like Jesus did.

Setting the Tone: Respect, Love, and Open Conversations

Before we dive into the chapters ahead, I want to set the tone for this journey. Think of this book as a safe space— a place where you can learn, ask questions, and even laugh along the way

We're going to keep things real and honest, but always with love and respect for God, for each other, and for ourselves.

Talking about our bodies, boundaries, and relationships doesn't need to feel awkward or scary; it's actually a way to celebrate the amazing people God made us to be.

In this book, you're encouraged to ask questions, reflect on your experiences, and maybe even start some conversations with your parents or other trusted adults.

Sometimes, you might read something that feels a little new or different. That's okay! Learning about ourselves and God's design is a process, and you don't need to understand everything all at once.

My Prayer for You

As we start this journey together, I want you to know that I am praying for each one of you.

I pray that this book will help you see how truly special you are and how much God loves you.

I pray that you'll feel safe, valued, and curious as we talk about these important topics. And most of all, I pray that you'll know you are never alone— God is with you, and He has a beautiful plan for your life.

Let's jump in and discover what God has to say about the amazing people He created us to be

Sharon L. Taylor

CHAPTER ONE

God's Amazing Design for Our Bodies

Created in God's Image: How We Reflect God's Beauty and Love

Hello there! I want you to take a moment and think about something amazing: you were made in God's image.

I know that phrase, "made in God's image," might seem hard to understand, especially when you think about it for the first time. Does it mean that God looks like us? Not exactly! But being created in God's image is something even more special and wonderful than just appearances.

When the Bible says that God made humans in His image, it means He made us with the ability to show love, kindness, creativity, and so many of the beautiful qualities that He has. Just think about that!

Out of all the things God made—flowers, mountains, stars, and animals—only humans were made in His image.

That means every time you show kindness to a friend, take care of your pet, create a beautiful piece of art, or even solve a tricky math problem, you are reflecting God's incredible creativity, wisdom, and love.

17

What Being Made in God's Image Means in Everyday Life

Sometimes, people think about themselves only in terms of what they can do or what they look like. But God sees us so differently.

Imagine this: God sees you as His beautiful creation, someone He loves deeply and unconditionally. He sees your strengths, your talents, and even the things that make you unique.

And because we're made in His image, each of us has a purpose and a reason for being here, just as we are.

Have you ever looked in the mirror and wondered about why you look the way you do? Maybe you have curly hair while your friend has straight hair. Maybe you're tall and someone else is shorter.

These differences are intentional, part of how God made each of us special. In the Bible, God tells us that He knows every detail about us—even the number of hairs on our head!

When you start to see yourself as God sees you, you'll begin to understand that you're more than just what you look like. You are a reflection of God's love, His creativity, and His purpose.

Learning to See Others as Made in God's Image, Too

Seeing ourselves as God's creation helps us understand something just as important: everyone else is also made in God's image.

That includes people who look different, act differently, or have different backgrounds. Each person reflects a part of God's creativity and beauty. So when we show kindness, love, and respect to others, we're honoring God in a big way.

As we move forward in this book, keep in mind that you're not just a body going through changes—you're a whole, beautiful person created by God, with a purpose and plan that only you can fulfill. Isn't that incredible?

Appreciating Our Bodies: Understanding the Wonder of God's Creation

Now that we know we're made in God's image, let's talk a little more about our bodies.

God didn't just create us in His image and then leave us on our own; He gave us these amazing, complex bodies that can do incredible things.

I don't just mean things like running fast or jumping high, but also things like thinking, feeling, and experiencing the world in a way that's unique to each of us.

The Science and Wonder of How We're Made

Let's take a look at some amazing facts about our bodies!

Did you know that your brain has more connections than there are stars in the Milky Way galaxy?

Or that your heart pumps enough blood in one day to fill up a large swimming pool? Your body is designed with purpose, function, and even a bit of mystery. And all of these things point back to the incredible wisdom of God.

Our bodies were also designed to grow and change over time. From the time you were a tiny baby, your body has been constantly working to help you become the person you are today.

And it's still doing that—your muscles, bones, and even your brain are all growing and changing.

This isn't by accident; it's part of God's amazing plan for us. Every time you take a breath, every time you learn something new, and even every time you skin your knee and it heals, you're experiencing the wonder of God's creation.

Learning to Appreciate Ourselves as We Are

I know that sometimes it can be hard to appreciate our bodies, especially if we feel different or if we wish we looked a certain way. But when you remember that your body is part of God's design, you start to see yourself in a new light.

Instead of focusing on things you might want to change, you can start to appreciate all the things your body can do. Every part of you is there for a reason, and God knew exactly what He was doing when He made you.

If you're ever tempted to think that you're not enough or that you need to be someone else, remember that you're already exactly who God wants you to be.

You don't need to look or act like anyone else to have value. God sees you as precious and wonderful just as you are, and learning to see yourself that way is part of learning to appreciate His work.

The Differences Between Boys and Girls: How God Made Us Special and Unique

One of the incredible things about God's creation is that He made boys and girls with special, unique qualities. These differences aren't mistakes or coincidences; they're part of

God's perfect plan. He made boys and girls to complement each other, with different strengths and gifts that make us better together.

Understanding Differences as Part of God's Plan

Think about this: in the Bible, God uses both men and women in powerful ways. He used men like Moses and David to lead His people, but He also used women like Esther and Ruth to show bravery and faithfulness.

In the same way, God created boys and girls today with different qualities that make each of us special. Boys might generally be stronger in some areas, while girls might be stronger in others.

These differences aren't meant to separate us or make one better than the other; they're meant to help us appreciate each other and work together.

But remember, these differences aren't just about physical traits. Boys and girls can both be smart, brave, kind, and talented. God gives each of us our own strengths and talents, and those strengths are meant to be shared. By appreciating our differences, we can work together to accomplish even more than we could on our own.

Learning to Celebrate Each Other's Uniqueness

Instead of focusing on comparing ourselves to others, we can start to see those differences as reasons to celebrate. When we remember that God made both boys and girls as part of His plan, we can treat each other with respect and appreciation.

Every time you see a friend who's different from you, remember that they are a special part of God's creation, just like you. We're all in this together, and our differences make life richer and more interesting.

Learning to Care for Our Bodies as a Way to Honor God

Finally, let's talk about something important: taking care of ourselves. One of the best ways to show gratitude for the bodies God gave us is by treating them with respect and love.

When we see our bodies as gifts from God, it changes how we think about things like food, exercise, rest, and even the words we say about ourselves.

Taking care of ourselves isn't just about feeling good or looking a certain way; it's about honoring God with the choices we make every day.

Seeing Self-Care as Worship

Let's think of self-care as a kind of worship. Worship isn't just singing songs or praying at church; it's also in the way we live and how we use the bodies God gave us.

When we choose to take care of ourselves, we're saying, "Thank you, God, for this amazing body!" We're respecting the temple He gave us and recognizing that we are important to Him.

Imagine you were given a beautiful, delicate gift from someone you love. You'd probably handle it with care, make sure it stays clean and protected, and treat it as something valuable.

That's how God wants us to treat ourselves. He cares about how we feel, how we grow, and even how much rest we get. Treating our bodies with kindness, we're respecting the gift that God gave us and showing our gratitude for His love.

Eating and Exercising with Purpose

One of the main ways we honor God with our bodies is by giving them what they need to be healthy and strong.

Eating healthy foods is a great start. Think of food as fuel for your body—just like a car needs gas, our bodies need nutritious foods to give us energy and help us grow. Eating fruits, vegetables, proteins, and whole grains keeps us strong and ready for all the amazing things God has planned for us.

Exercise is another important way to take care of ourselves. Playing outside, riding your bike, dancing, or even walking helps keep your body active and healthy. When we move our bodies, we're not only staying strong, but we're also keeping our hearts and minds healthy.

God designed us to move, giving us muscles and bones that grow stronger when we use them. Exercise doesn't have to be a chore or something we dread.

It can be fun! Think of activities you enjoy, whether it's playing sports, running around with friends, or taking nature hikes. When you enjoy movement, it's easier to make exercise a regular part of your life—and you'll feel good about taking care of the body God gave you.

The Importance of Rest and Relaxation

Alongside movement, rest is just as important. Just as God rested on the seventh day after creating the world, He wants us to take time to rest, too. Rest helps our bodies recover, recharge, and be ready for what's next.

Sometimes, we might feel like we need to keep going and doing things all the time. But rest is a way to honor God by taking time to slow down, relax, and enjoy peace. This can mean getting a good night's sleep, taking short breaks during the day, or spending quiet time praying and reflecting.

When we take time to rest, we're giving our minds a chance to slow down and our bodies a chance to rebuild. Think of sleep as a way of hitting the "reset" button every night.

While we sleep, our brains organize what we've learned, and our bodies repair themselves. When we wake up feeling refreshed, we're ready to take on a new day and all the exciting things God has planned for us.

Choosing Words of Kindness Toward Ourselves

Honoring God with our bodies isn't just about what we do; it's also about what we say and think about ourselves. Sometimes, it can be easy to think negative thoughts, like "I wish I looked different" or "I'm not as strong as someone else." But remember, God created you exactly the way you are for a reason.

Every time we say something positive about ourselves or thank God for the body we have, we're choosing to see ourselves the way He does— with love and kindness.

If you ever catch yourself thinking unkind thoughts about your body, try to replace them with words that honor the amazing creation you are. Instead of "I'm not good enough," try saying, "I am made in God's image, and He loves me just as I am."

When you start treating yourself with kindness, you'll notice a difference. You'll feel more at peace, more confident, and closer to God, knowing you're seeing yourself the way He does.

Serving Others Through Self-Care

One of the incredible things about taking care of ourselves is that it helps us care for others, too.

When we're healthy, strong, and rested, we're better able to help our families, serve our friends, and be kind to those around us. Jesus often spoke about loving others, and part of that love is being ready and able to serve.

Self-care is never selfish; it's actually a way of preparing ourselves to be our best for the people God puts in our lives. When we eat well, rest, and take care of our mental health, we're able to show up as our best selves, ready to share God's love and kindness with others.

So, as you think about taking care of yourself, remember that you're doing it for more than just yourself. You're honoring God, respecting the gift He gave you, and preparing to serve others with joy and energy.

Taking care of your body isn't just about looking after yourself—it's part of how you're preparing to make a difference in the world, one small step at a time.

Practical Ways to Honor God with Our Bodies Every Day

Start with Gratitude: Each morning, take a moment to thank God for the gift of your body.

Think about something specific you're grateful for, whether it's your strength, your ability to think and learn, or the energy you have to play.

Make Healthy Choices: As you go through your day, try to make small choices that honor your body. Choose foods that give you energy, move around when you can, and take breaks to rest when you're tired.

Speak Kindly to Yourself: Whenever you notice negative thoughts, gently remind yourself that you're made in God's image and that He loves you just as you are. Speak words of kindness and gratitude over yourself.

Enjoy Time in God's Creation: Spend time outdoors, whether you're playing, going for a walk, or simply sitting and enjoying nature.

Being outside helps us remember that our bodies are part of God's creation and that we're connected to the world He made.

Pray for Guidance and Strength: Ask God to help you take care of yourself in ways that honor Him. Pray for wisdom to make good choices and for strength when you feel tired or unsure.

Honoring our bodies, we're honoring God and showing Him that we're grateful for the gift He's given us. Remember, your body is a temple, and you are wonderfully made.

As you learn to care for yourself, you're not just making good choices; you're growing in faith, learning to appreciate God's creation, and becoming a stronger, healthier person ready to share God's love with the world around you.

CHAPTER TWO

Why Boundaries Matter: How They Keep Us Safe and Show Love for Ourselves and Others

Let's start with an idea that might feel pretty simple at first: boundaries.

When we hear the word "boundary," we might picture a fence around a yard or lines on a soccer field, right?

These boundaries are there to show us where it's safe to go or where the game rules apply. Boundaries work in a similar way in our lives.

They help us stay safe, respect others, and live in a way that honors God. I know it may sound surprising, but boundaries are one of the most loving things we can set for ourselves and others.

Now, let's think about it this way: God created each of us uniquely, and He also created us to live in a world where we're connected to each other.

We have family, friends, teachers, and teammates, all of whom we interact with every day. Boundaries help us know how to interact with these people in a way that shows kindness, respect, and understanding.

They allow us to protect what matters to us and ensure that we're treated with the same respect we offer others.

God's Example of Boundaries

Boundaries are a part of God's design, and we can see this in the Bible.

When God gave the Ten Commandments to Moses, for example, He was giving His people guidelines on how to live and treat each other.

These commandments were essentially God's boundaries—ways to live that honor Him and respect others. When we think of boundaries as part of God's plan, it becomes clear that they're not about restricting us or making life harder; they're about creating a safe, loving, and respectful world.

Why Boundaries Are Loving and Necessary

Sometimes, it's easy to think that boundaries are about saying "no" or pushing others away.

But in reality, setting boundaries is a way to care for yourself and the people around you. Imagine you're playing a game, but no one follows any rules.

People might start bumping into each other, getting frustrated, or even getting hurt.

Boundaries are like the rules in the game—they help us understand how to interact safely and fairly with each other. Boundaries are also a way of showing love. When we have boundaries, we respect our time, our bodies, and our feelings.

For instance, saying "I need some time alone" is a way of honoring your need for rest, and it helps others understand that this time is important to you.

Setting a boundary is not selfish—it's a way of caring for yourself so that you can be your best self with others.

A Loving Reminder

As you go through life, you'll see that different people have different boundaries. Some people may love big hugs, while others prefer a wave or a smile.

Just as we want others to respect our personal space and choices, it's important that we do the same for them. When we honor each other's boundaries, we're actually practicing love and kindness.

Setting Healthy Boundaries with Friends, Family, and Others

Boundaries aren't just important in theory; they're something we practice in all of our relationships.

Whether we're with family, friends, or people we meet at school or church, setting boundaries helps us create positive connections.

And the great thing about boundaries is that we can adjust them as we grow and as we get to know people better.

Boundaries with Family

Let's start with the people closest to us—our families. Family relationships are often filled with love and support, but we also need boundaries within them.

For example, you might love your sibling dearly but also need some quiet time after a long day.

You could say, "I'd love to hang out later, but I need some alone time first."

This doesn't mean you don't love your sibling—it just shows that you recognize your needs and want to be able to enjoy time together when you're ready.

Setting boundaries with family members can sometimes feel challenging because they're the people we're around the most, and they know us so well.

But remember, even Jesus sometimes took time alone to pray and recharge.

God understands that we all need moments to rest and take care of ourselves, and it's okay to let our family know what we need.

Boundaries with Friends

Boundaries are also important in our friendships. Good friends are a wonderful gift from God, but even in these relationships, we need to set boundaries to keep them healthy.

Maybe you have a friend who wants to talk all the time, but you sometimes feel overwhelmed or need a break.

It's okay to say, "I love talking with you, but I need a little time to focus on something else." A good friend will understand and respect your need for space.

Friendships grow stronger when we respect each other's boundaries.

And remember, setting boundaries with friends isn't about rejecting them—it's about creating a balanced relationship where both of you feel safe and respected.

By communicating your needs and listening to theirs, you're helping to build a friendship based on honesty and kindness.

Boundaries with Others Sometimes, we have to set boundaries with people we don't know as well.

Maybe there's someone at school who asks a lot of questions about your personal life, or someone who stands too close and makes you feel uncomfortable.

It's perfectly okay to let them know, kindly, that you prefer a bit more space or that some topics are private.

You can say, "I'd rather not talk about that right now," or simply step back if someone is too close. In all of these situations, remember that boundaries aren't about putting up walls—they're about creating space where you feel respected and safe. Setting boundaries is part of growing up and learning to interact with others in a way that honors both yourself and the people around you.

What the Bible Teaches About Respecting Our Own and Others' Boundaries

Throughout the Bible, we see examples of how God wants us to treat others with respect and kindness.

One of the clearest examples is the Golden Rule, which says, "Do to others what you would have them do to you" (Matthew 7:12). This means treating others the way you'd like to be treated, and respecting boundaries is one way we can do this.

Respecting Our Own Boundaries

Respecting our own boundaries is an important part of respecting the person God made us to be.

God gave each of us unique talents, strengths, and even weaknesses, and He wants us to honor who we are.

When we respect our boundaries—whether it's taking time to rest, saying "no" to things that make us uncomfortable, or choosing friends who support us—we are honoring God's design for our lives.

Think of boundaries as a way to protect the things that matter most to you, like your faith, your values, and your personal comfort.

God doesn't want us to ignore our feelings or pretend everything is okay when it's not. Instead, He encourages us to speak up and communicate our needs in a way that is honest and loving.

Respecting Others' Boundaries

Just as we respect our own boundaries, it's equally important to respect the boundaries of others. In Philippians 2:4, we read, "Let each of you look not only to his own interests, but also to the interests of others."

This means we should think about how our actions affect others and make sure we're treating them with the same respect we hope to receive.

When we respect others' boundaries, we show that we care about them as individuals and value their comfort and well-being.

If a friend tells you they need some time alone, try to understand and give them that space.

If a family member asks for help but you're not sure what to do, listening and respecting their wishes shows that you're there for them in a way that honors their needs.

Learning to Say "No": Practicing Consent in a Respectful Way One of the most important parts of setting boundaries is learning to say "no."

This can feel challenging at first, especially if we don't want to hurt someone's feelings or feel pressured to go along with what others want.

But saying "no" when we need to is actually a way to practice respect for ourselves and for others.

Why Saying "No" is Sometimes Necessary Saying "no" doesn't mean you don't care about others—it simply means you're recognizing what's right for you in that moment.

If someone asks you to do something that makes you uncomfortable or goes against your values, saying "no" is a way to stand up for yourself and the person God created you to be.

God doesn't want us to go along with things that hurt us or compromise our beliefs. Instead, He gives us the courage to make choices that reflect His love and wisdom.

Using "No" to Practice Consent

Consent means agreeing to something willingly and feeling comfortable with that decision.

When we say "yes," it should always be because we genuinely want to, not because we feel pressured or afraid to say "no."

Practicing consent is about making choices that honor God's plan for us and respect the choices of others. If someone asks you to do something that feels wrong or uncomfortable, remember that you have the right to say "no." It's okay to stand firm in your beliefs and let others know when something doesn't feel right.

By practicing consent and respecting our own boundaries, we're showing that we trust God's guidance and have confidence in the choices He's leading us to make.

How to Say "No" Respectfully

Sometimes, saying "no" is as simple as saying, "I'd rather not," or "That doesn't feel right to me." The important thing is to communicate clearly and kindly.

When we say "no" with respect, we're honoring both ourselves and the other person.

We don't need to be rude or harsh; we can simply be honest about what we feel comfortable with. And believe it or not, most people will appreciate your honesty because it shows that you're being true to yourself.

Let's say a friend invites you to do something you're not sure about. You can say, "Thank you for inviting me, but I'm going to pass this time."

Or, if you feel pressured to share something personal and you're not ready, try saying, "I don't feel comfortable talking about that right now."

It's a gentle way to set a boundary without hurting anyone's feelings, and it reminds others to respect your comfort zone.

Finding the Right Words

When we're learning to set boundaries and practice consent, it helps to have a few go-to phrases that make it easier to say "no."

Some good examples include:

Practice Makes Perfect

Like anything else, learning to say "no" takes practice. At first, it might feel awkward or uncomfortable, and that's okay. Start by setting small boundaries with people you trust, like family members or close friends.

Over time, you'll become more comfortable setting boundaries in all areas of your life.

With each step, you're not only honoring your own needs but also setting an example of how to respect others' boundaries.

When we build relationships on clear, honest communication, we create space for everyone to feel valued and safe.

And that's what God desires for each of us—that we live in relationships that are respectful, loving, and full of kindness.

40

Sharon L. Taylor

CHAPTER THREE

God's Plan for Relationships Friendship, Family, and Love in God's View

As we begin exploring God's plan for relationships, I want you to imagine a world where we're all connected— where friends, family, and loved ones surround us, each bringing something special into our lives.

In the Bible, God teaches us a lot about relationships, showing us that He values every connection we have.

Whether it's the love of our family, the encouragement of friends, or even the kindness we show to people we meet, each relationship is an opportunity to share God's love.

Now, I know relationships can sometimes feel complicated, especially as we grow up and meet new people.

You might wonder what makes a friendship healthy or how to handle differences with family members.

The good news is that the Bible offers us a guide to help us understand these relationships and how we can navigate them in a way that honors God and strengthens our connection with Him.

God's Purpose for Relationships In the very beginning, God said, "It is not good for the man to be alone" (Genesis 2:18).

He created us to live in community with others, to share in each other's joys and challenges. Relationships aren't just about filling our lives with people; they're about learning how to love, serve, and support each other.

God designed friendships and family connections to help us grow, to bring joy into our lives, and to reflect His love. Relationships also shape who we are.

They encourage us to become better, to think of others, and to learn patience and kindness.

Have you ever noticed how spending time with positive, loving people makes you feel more hopeful and joyful?

That's the power of a God-centered relationship. It builds us up and makes us stronger.

Different Types of Love in the Bible

The Bible talks about many types of love.

For example, there's **philia** , which is the love we feel for friends.

Think of David and Jonathan, whose friendship was so strong that they stood by each other in good times and bad.

Then there's **storge** , the love of family members, like the love between Ruth and Naomi, who were there for each other through loss and challenges.

And of course, there's **agape** —God's unconditional love for us.

This is the deepest love, the one that reminds us that we're cherished no matter what.

God's love is our example of how we should love others. When we approach relationships with this kind of love, we're patient, forgiving, and respectful, just as God is with us.

And by learning to love in these ways, we're honoring God's design for relationships.

Respect, Kindness, and Caring for Others

In every relationship, whether it's with family, friends, or even classmates, God calls us to show respect and kindness. Respect means recognizing the value of each person God created, treating them as unique and important.

Kindness, on the other hand, is about showing care, compassion, and understanding. Together, respect and kindness form the foundation of healthy relationships.

The Golden Rule: A Guide to Kindness

One of the best guides we have for treating others well is the Golden Rule: "Do to others what you would have them do to you" (Matthew 7:12).

This simple principle helps us think about how our actions and words affect others. If we want others to treat us with respect and kindness, we should start by showing that same respect and kindness to them.

Imagine you're in a situation where a friend feels left out. What would you want someone to do for you if you were in their shoes?

Wouldn't you want a friend to come over and make you feel included?

Following the Golden Rule helps us become the kind of friend or family member others can rely on.

And as we practice kindness, we're not only honoring our relationships but also bringing a little bit of God's love into each interaction.

Choosing Words Wisely

Another part of showing respect and kindness is choosing our words carefully. Words have the power to build others up or tear them down.

Proverbs 16:24 reminds us, "Gracious words are like honeycomb, sweetness to the soul and health to the body." When we speak with kindness, we're offering something valuable and meaningful to others.

Sometimes, it's easy to forget how much our words matter, especially in moments of frustration or impatience.

But even in challenging times, God encourages us to respond with love. If you find yourself in a tough moment with a friend or sibling, take a deep breath and think about what you want to say.

Ask yourself if your words are loving and respectful.

It might be hard at first, but as you practice, you'll find that choosing kind words becomes a habit that strengthens your relationships.

Caring Through Actions

Showing respect and kindness goes beyond words—it's about actions, too.

When we help someone, offer a listening ear, or show patience, we're caring for them in a meaningful way. God calls us to care for each other's needs, to lend a hand when someone is struggling, and to be a source of comfort and support.

This doesn't mean we have to do everything for everyone, but it does mean being there when we can.

Think about Jesus as an example. He was always willing to listen, to help, and to encourage others. He cared for people not just with words, but with His actions. By following His example, we can make a real difference in the lives of those we love.

Choosing Friends Who Encourage You to Live in Faith

Friendships are a gift from God, and they can be one of the greatest sources of joy, support, and encouragement in our lives. However, friendships also have a powerful influence on who we are and who we become.

The Bible says, "As iron sharpens iron, so one person sharpens another" (Proverbs 27:17), meaning that good friends help us grow in our faith and become stronger in character.

What Makes a Good Friend?

A good friend is someone who encourages you, respects you, and shares similar values. They're the ones who help you stay true to yourself and your beliefs, and who make you feel safe and valued.

Think about the friends in your life who make you feel loved and accepted.

These are the friends who celebrate your successes and support you during challenges.

They're like the friends who carried their paralyzed friend to Jesus because they wanted him to be healed (Mark 2:1-12).

That's true friendship—people who bring us closer to God. When we surround ourselves with friends who encourage us to live in faith, we're more likely to make choices that honor God. These friends remind us of our values, support us in our faith journey, and help us become the best versions of ourselves.

Making Faith-Based Choices in Friendships

Sometimes, it's tempting to follow friends who might make choices that don't align with our faith.

Maybe they pressure you to do things that make you uncomfortable, or perhaps they don't respect your boundaries. It's okay to have friends who think differently, but it's also important to protect your own beliefs and values.

If you ever feel that a friend is leading you away from God, it's okay to take a step back and reflect on what's best for you.

This doesn't mean you have to end the friendship, but you may need to set boundaries to ensure that you're staying true to your values. Remember, God wants us to surround ourselves with people who bring out the best in us.

Recognizing Godly vs. Harmful Relationships: Knowing When to Seek Help

Not all relationships are healthy or positive, and it's important to know the difference between those that build us up and those that bring us down.

A godly relationship is one that aligns with God's principles, shows respect, and encourages us to grow in our faith. A harmful relationship, on the other hand, might involve someone who disrespects us, pressures us to do things we're uncomfortable with, or makes us feel small.

Signs of a Godly Relationship

A godly relationship is one where you feel respected, valued, and supported. In these relationships, both people care about each other's well-being and want what's best for each other.

They're patient, kind, and willing to listen, just as we're called to be in 1 Corinthians 13. When you're around these people, you feel safe and uplifted.

You know that they respect your boundaries and encourage you to be the person God created you to be.

Recognizing Harmful Relationships

On the other hand, harmful relationships can feel stressful, hurtful, or even scary.

If someone is constantly pressuring you, putting you down, or ignoring your boundaries, that's a sign that the relationship might not be healthy.

Proverbs 22:24-25 warns us to "not make friends with a hot-tempered person, do not associate with one easily angered," because negative influences can lead us down a path we don't want to go.

If you find yourself in a relationship that feels harmful, don't be afraid to reach out for help.

Talk to a trusted adult—maybe a parent, teacher, or pastor—who can give you guidance and support.

God never wants us to feel unsafe or disrespected in our relationships, and there are always people who can help us find a way forward.

Seeking God's Guidance in Relationships

Whenever you're uncertain about a relationship, remember that God is there to guide you.

Pray for wisdom and strength to make the right choices, and trust that He will help you surround yourself with people who honor and support you.

Sometimes, our emotions can cloud our judgment, especially when it comes to friendships or relationships that feel complicated or confusing.

That's why inviting God into your decision-making is so important—He understands the bigger picture and knows what's best for you, even when it's not immediately clear.

When you pray, ask God to give you insight into whether a relationship is helping or hurting you.

Ask Him to reveal the true nature of that friendship or connection, and to give you peace about the steps you need to take. God's guidance isn't always immediate, but if you listen closely, He will show you signs. It might be a feeling of peace when you're around certain people, or a sense of discomfort around others.

He might send someone to give you wise advice or open doors to new friendships that reflect His love.

Trusting God's Timing in Friendships

Sometimes, relationships change over time, and it can be painful when a close friendship begins to fade or shift.

It's natural to feel sad or even disappointed when this happens. However, trusting that God has a plan—even in these moments—can give us comfort.

He might be preparing you for new friendships, or He could be using this experience to help you grow stronger and wiser.

God brings people into our lives for specific reasons, and sometimes only for a season.

Perhaps there's something important you were meant to learn from that friendship, or maybe you helped each other during a difficult time. Trust that, whether a friendship continues or comes to an end, God's purpose for that relationship was meaningful.

Keeping Your Heart Open to New Relationships

When we experience friendship changes or difficult relationships, it can be tempting to close ourselves off from others to protect our hearts. But remember that God encourages us to keep an open heart, to be willing to trust and connect with others in a way that brings joy and reflects His love.

Each new friendship is an opportunity to grow and learn more about yourself and the kind of friend you want to be. Embrace the friendships that bring you closer to God, and be open to meeting new people who share your values.

You might be surprised at how God uses these connections to shape you in ways you never expected.

Trust that, through each relationship, He is helping you build a community of love, respect, and faith. And always remember, you are never alone—God is with you in every relationship, guiding you, strengthening you, and helping you become the friend, sibling, and person He created you to be.

Sharon L. Taylor

CHAPTER FOUR

Introduction to Biblical Sexuality God's Design for Sexuality: Why It's a Gift for Marriage

When I first started learning about God's design for sexuality, I remember feeling both curious and a little uncertain.

Growing up, we hear many things about love and relationships, and sometimes it can feel confusing to understand how all these pieces fit together.

But what if I told you that God has an amazing plan for love, relationships, and sexuality—one that's designed to protect us, give us joy, and bring us closer to Him?

In the Bible, we see that God created each of us with unique bodies, hearts, and minds, and part of His beautiful plan includes the gift of sexuality.

But sexuality isn't just about physical feelings; it's about connection, commitment, and the kind of love that God designed to be shared in marriage between a man and a woman.

The Bible describes marriage as a sacred bond between two people (**man and woman**) who choose to love, support, and cherish each other. It's a relationship that mirrors God's own commitment to us and His deep, unchanging love.

When we talk about sexuality as a gift for marriage, we're recognizing that this is something God gave to us with a purpose.

Just like any special gift, He wants us to understand its value and treat it with care.

This allows us to experience love and connection in a way that's healthy, respectful, and joyful—just the way God intended.

Understanding Love vs. Romantic Love: Age-Appropriate Insights

Love is a big word, isn't it?

We hear it in movies, read about it in books, and see it all around us. But love isn't just one thing; it comes in many forms.

As we grow, we start to experience different kinds of love—love for family, love for friends, and even the beginning of what we might call "romantic love."

Understanding the difference between these kinds of love is important, especially as you think about what God teaches us about relationships.

The Difference Between Friendship Love and Romantic Love

Friendship love, or philia , is about connection and shared interests. It's the love you feel for a friend you enjoy spending time with or a family member you care about deeply.

This type of love brings people together, helps us feel connected, and builds trust. When God gives us friends and family, He's blessing us with people who help us grow and learn, and who remind us of the joy of companionship. Romantic love, however, is a different experience.

This kind of love includes deeper feelings and often a desire to be especially close to someone.

But these feelings can be powerful and sometimes confusing. Romantic love is natural, but it's also a feeling that God designed to be a special part of marriage.

In marriage, romantic love becomes part of a committed relationship built on trust, respect, and shared values.

It's a love that grows over time and becomes even stronger as two people continue to care for each other through both good times and challenges.

When Is Romantic Love Appropriate?

At your age, it's normal to feel curious about romantic love, but it's also important to remember that these feelings are meant to be explored slowly and thoughtfully.

God's plan includes allowing these emotions to develop when we're ready for the commitment that comes with them.

That's why, as young people, our main focus can be on building friendships and learning what it means to be a kind, supportive, and faithful friend.

These friendships help prepare us for the relationships we'll have in the future and help us understand the difference between healthy love and mere attraction.

Respecting Our Own and Others' Bodies as Holy and Precious

God created each of us with a body that's unique, beautiful, and full of purpose. The Bible tells us that our bodies are "temples of the Holy Spirit" (1 Corinthians 6:19).

This means that our bodies are precious and deserve to be treated with respect and care. Just as we wouldn't mistreat a beautiful church or building, God calls us to treat our own bodies, and the bodies of others, with honor.

What Does It Mean to Respect Our Bodies?

Respecting our bodies means understanding that they are valuable and worth protecting. It means making choices that keep us healthy, like eating well, getting enough sleep, and avoiding things that could harm us.

When we choose to care for our bodies, we're saying "thank you" to God for the incredible creation He's given us.

Respecting our bodies also means setting boundaries to protect ourselves and others. Boundaries are like invisible lines that help us stay safe and feel comfortable.

For example, if you don't feel ready to talk about something personal or uncomfortable, you have the right to say "no" or "not right now." Boundaries remind us to treat others with respect, too, by honoring their choices and not pressuring them to do things they aren't comfortable with.

Seeing Others as Precious to God

Just as our own bodies are holy and precious, so are the bodies of others. Each person we meet is created by God, loved by Him, and deserving of respect.

This means treating others with kindness, being gentle with their feelings, and understanding that their boundaries are important too.

When we honor other people's bodies and boundaries, we show God's love to them and reflect His values in our actions.

Why Waiting is God's Plan: Emphasizing Purity in a Positive, Supportive Way

Waiting might seem like a big ask, especially when we live in a world that often tells us that love and romance should happen quickly. But God's plan is a bit different.

He calls us to be patient and to wait until marriage to experience the full expression of love and sexuality.

This isn't because God wants to deny us something good; it's because He wants to protect us and ensure we experience the beauty of love in its best and healthiest form.

Why Does God Ask Us to Wait?

In the Bible, God asks us to wait because He understands the deep importance of commitment and trust.

Marriage is a promise between two people to love and support each other for life, and it's in this safe, committed relationship that we can experience the gift of sexuality as He intended.

Waiting until marriage allows us to experience love without fear, shame, or regret, knowing that we're following God's design.

Purity as a Positive Choice

Choosing to wait and pursue purity isn't about saying "no" to love—it's about saying "yes" to God's best plan for you. Purity is a decision to respect yourself, to honor your body, and to hold out for the kind of love that's built on commitment and faithfulness.

Purity isn't just about avoiding certain actions; it's about developing a heart that desires to follow God and trust His guidance.

I like to think of purity as a journey of becoming the person God created you to be.

It means learning to value yourself, to make choices that reflect your worth, and to surround yourself with friends who encourage you to stay true to your values.

And the amazing thing is, God walks with us on this journey. He understands our struggles, He knows our hearts, and He's there to help us make choices that honor Him.

Waiting as a Strength

Sometimes, waiting can feel challenging. You might wonder why it's necessary or feel curious about romance and relationships.

Remember that choosing to wait doesn't make you "weird" or "old-fashioned." Instead, it shows a strength and wisdom that not everyone has.

It shows that you're choosing to trust God's plan, even when it's different from what others might do.

Waiting is a way of saying, "I believe that God's plan is good, and I trust Him to bring the right person into my life at the right time." In the end, God's plan for sexuality, love, and relationships is one that reflects His deep love for us. By understanding His design and making choices that align with it, we're honoring Him and building a future that's filled with respect, joy, and genuine love.

CHAPTER FIVE

Dealing with Peer Pressure and Media Influence What is Peer Pressure?

Identifying Unhealthy Influence

When I was younger, I remember feeling like I always wanted to fit in with my friends. That's something I think we all experience because it's natural to want to belong and feel accepted.

But as we grow, we also start noticing moments when fitting in might mean doing things we're unsure about or going against what we know is right.

This is what we call "peer pressure." Peer pressure happens when friends, classmates, or even people we see on social media try to influence us to act a certain way or make certain choices, even if they don't say it outright.

It could be something big, like being pressured to say or do things that go against our values, or it could be smaller things, like feeling like you have to dress or act a certain way to feel accepted.

Sometimes, peer pressure is obvious—like when someone tells you directly to do something.

But it can also be subtle, like feeling you need to go along with something just because everyone else is doing it.

Let's take a deeper look at what unhealthy influence looks like and how we can recognize it.

Imagine, for instance, that some friends start sharing gossip about others.

Even if they don't directly tell you to join in, you might feel tempted because you don't want to be left out.

In cases like these, it's important to remember that just because "everyone else is doing it" doesn't mean you have to as well.

God calls us to live in a way that reflects kindness, honesty, and respect for others, so when we recognize that an action or conversation doesn't align with these values, it's a sign that we may need to step back.

One of the best things you can do is learn to recognize your own values and stay true to them. It's okay if what's popular doesn't match what feels right to you.

Part of growing up is realizing that not every voice we hear is wise or good, and sometimes it's necessary to step back and make choices based on what God would want for us.

Remember, your friends and the people around you aren't the ones who define your worth—only God does.

Practicing Self-Respect When Facing Peer Pressure

Facing peer pressure can feel tough, especially when it involves people we look up to or care about. I know that in moments like these, it's easy to feel torn.

You might wonder, "What will my friends think if I don't go along with this?" But here's something important to remember: choosing to act with self-respect is always worth it, even if it means standing out.

Self-respect is about valuing yourself and knowing that you deserve to make choices that honor who you are.

This doesn't mean that you won't feel pressured, but it means that you'll have the strength to choose what's best for you even when it's hard.

To practice self-respect, start by reminding yourself that you don't have to do anything just because someone else thinks you should.

God made you unique, and He gave you a sense of right and wrong for a reason.

One way to build self-respect is by thinking about your boundaries ahead of time.

For example, if you know that certain topics or activities make you uncomfortable, decide now that you'll politely decline if they come up.

You can even practice saying phrases like, "No, I'd rather not," or "I'm not interested in that." Having responses ready can make it easier to stand firm when the moment comes.

It's also helpful to remember that choosing to walk away doesn't mean you're judging others or that you're "uncool." It just means that you're choosing to live in a way that honors your values.

The people who truly care about you will respect your boundaries, even if they don't agree with every choice you make. And by practicing self-respect, you'll also inspire others to make choices that align with their own values. God calls us to be a light for others, and sometimes the best way to do that is by simply living in a way that shows you respect yourself.

Media and Body Image: How to See Ourselves Through God's Loving Eyes

If there's one thing I've noticed, it's that we're surrounded by images and messages about how we're supposed to look.

Social media, TV, movies, and even advertisements all seem to have a certain "look" or "style" that they push.

This can sometimes make us feel like we need to change who we are to be "good enough" or "attractive."

But let me share something I've learned: no one has the right to tell you what you need to look like to be valuable. God created each of us in His image, and He sees us as perfectly and wonderfully made.

In Psalm 139, the Bible tells us that we are "fearfully and wonderfully made," and that each of us is God's unique creation. When we start comparing ourselves to people in the media, we forget that God doesn't use the world's standards to measure our beauty. Instead, He looks at our hearts and sees our kindness, our faithfulness, and the love we share with others.

If you ever feel unsure about your appearance, try reminding yourself of how God sees you.

He created you just as you are, with your own special look, talents, and personality. No filter, no angle, and no number of "likes" can change that.

In fact, the very things that make you different are often the qualities God will use to make an impact on the world around you.

Finding Balance with Media

Sometimes, the messages we see online can make us feel pressured to look or act in ways that don't reflect who we truly are.

If you find yourself feeling down after scrolling through social media or watching certain shows, consider taking a break.

Think about what kind of messages lift you up and remind you of your value. Filling your mind with positive, uplifting content can help you see yourself as God does. Remember that God's view of you doesn't change based on your appearance or popularity. His love for you is deep and constant, and by focusing on that love, you can build a strong, healthy self-image that isn't shaken by the world's opinions.

Staying Rooted in Faith

When Influences Conflict with God's Teachings There's no doubt that living according to God's teachings can feel challenging, especially when the world around us promotes different ideas.

You might see things in media, hear things from friends, or read things online that don't line up with what the Bible says.

This can make you question your faith or wonder if following God's way is really possible.

Staying rooted in faith means remembering that God's wisdom is greater than any other voice. The Bible gives us guidance for a reason: it's God's way of helping us make choices that protect our hearts, minds, and futures.

Even when other influences conflict with His teachings, remember that His ways are designed for your good. He sees beyond the trends, the peer pressure, and the momentary temptations, and He knows the path that will lead you to true joy and peace.

Building a Strong Foundation in Faith

One way to stay grounded in faith is by regularly reading and reflecting on God's Word. Spending time in the Bible can remind you of God's love and strengthen your confidence to make choices that honor Him.

Verses like Proverbs 3:5-6, which encourage us to "Trust in the Lord with all your heart," remind us that God's wisdom is a source of strength, especially when we face difficult influences.

It can also help to talk to trusted family members, mentors, or friends who share your faith.

When we surround ourselves with people who support our beliefs, we feel more confident in our choices.

Whether it's a parent, youth leader, or close friend, having someone you can turn to for advice can make a big difference.

Choosing to Shine God's Light

When the world around us feels overwhelming, God calls us to be a light—to show love, kindness, and integrity, even when it's hard.

This doesn't mean we're perfect or that we never make mistakes, but it means that we aim to live in a way that reflects God's love.

Choosing to stay rooted in faith is like planting a strong tree: its roots go deep, and it stands tall even when the winds of peer pressure and media influence try to sway it. Remember, God is always with you, guiding you, strengthening you, and helping you stay true to the values He's placed in your heart.

When you rely on Him, you can navigate peer pressure, media influence, and any other challenges that come your way with confidence and grace.

And through it all, you'll discover that living in faith brings a joy and peace that nothing else can provide.

CHAPTER SIX

Communication with Parents and Trusted Adults The Importance of Talking Openly About Puberty and Boundaries

When I was your age, I remember how some topics felt hard to bring up with adults, even though I knew they were important.

It's normal to feel a bit awkward talking about things like puberty and boundaries, but here's something I've learned: open communication with people you trust can be one of the most comforting and helpful things you do as you grow up.

Talking to parents or trusted adults about these subjects doesn't just help you understand what's happening with your body and emotions; it also creates a foundation of trust.

When you're able to speak openly, it shows that you value their guidance, and it gives them the opportunity to be there for you in meaningful ways.

Sometimes we feel like adults won't understand, but you might be surprised.

They went through these changes once too, and most of them have probably felt the same mix of curiosity, confusion, and even nervousness you may be experiencing now.

When it comes to talking about boundaries, sharing your feelings is also incredibly valuable.

You're in a phase of life where you're beginning to figure out what makes you comfortable or uncomfortable, and communicating those feelings to others helps them respect your choices.

Learning to say, "I'm not okay with that," or "I'd rather talk about something else," can feel a bit intimidating, but it's a powerful way to honor yourself and invite others to honor you too.

For some kids, talking to parents feels natural. For others, it might feel a bit scary.

If you feel hesitant, try starting with something simple. You could say, "Mom, Dad, there's something I've been curious about.

Could we talk?" or "I read something today that made me think, and I'd like to hear what you think too."

Approaching them with curiosity and openness can make it easier to start the conversation. Most parents genuinely want to help, even if they sometimes seem busy or unsure of what to say at first.

By taking the first step to communicate openly, you're creating a bond of understanding and trust that will be helpful now and in the years to come.

How to Ask Questions and Share Feelings

Asking questions and sharing your feelings might sound simple, but it can actually be a big step.

Questions like, "What's happening to my body?" or "How do I handle my feelings?" are important, and expressing these thoughts helps you grow closer to the people who care about you.

You may find that some adults answer these questions easily, while others might feel just as awkward as you do.

But here's the great part—asking questions shows that you're curious, that you want to learn, and that you respect their guidance.

One way to get started is by writing down questions when they pop into your mind. Sometimes, when we're face- to-face with someone, it's easy to forget what we wanted to ask, so having a list can be helpful.

If you're nervous about starting a conversation, you can even show them your list. You might say, "I have a few things I've been wondering about.

Could you help me with these?" Remember, adults don't expect you to have all the answers or to know exactly what to ask. They just appreciate that you're taking the time to talk to them.

When it comes to sharing your feelings, be honest about how you're doing, even if it's not all "happy" emotions.

You could say, "I'm feeling a bit stressed about school," or "I'm a bit nervous about some of the changes I'm noticing." Opening up like this gives them a chance to offer comfort, advice, and sometimes even share their own experiences, which can help you feel less alone.

Sometimes, you may feel that adults don't quite understand what you're going through.

If that happens, be patient with them. You could try explaining your feelings a bit more or ask them how they felt at your age.

A lot of times, they'll remember their own experiences and be able to relate to you in ways you didn't expect.

Seeking Guidance and Wisdom from Christian Mentors

Aside from parents, having other trusted adults in your life, like Christian mentors, can be an incredible source of guidance. Mentors are often people who have a bit more life experience and a deep understanding of God's Word.

They might be youth leaders, teachers, or family friends who you look up to and feel comfortable talking to.

These are people who can offer you advice, help you navigate challenges, and give you a fresh perspective on what you're experiencing.

Mentors are great people to turn to for big questions, especially when you're looking for someone who can connect faith with everyday life.

They can help you explore what it means to follow God's plan during different stages of life, and they can give you insights on how to handle peer pressure, difficult choices, and even big emotions. Plus, because they're outside your immediate family, sometimes it feels a bit easier to talk with them about certain topics.

If you don't already have a mentor, you could pray for God to lead you to someone who can be there for you.

Sometimes mentors come into our lives through church groups, youth programs, or community activities. You might be drawn to someone because of their kindness, wisdom, or the way they live out their faith.

Once you find someone you trust, don't be afraid to reach out and let them know that you'd love to spend time learning from them.

Most people feel honored to share their experiences with younger friends, especially when it comes to growing in faith and understanding. When you have a mentor, you'll find that they're there to listen, to answer questions, and to help you make wise decisions.

Even if they don't have all the answers, they'll likely point you back to God's Word, helping you build your own foundation of faith.

Learning to Pray for God's Guidance in Relationships and Growing Up

One of the most beautiful things about our relationship with God is that we can come to Him for guidance anytime. When it comes to relationships, friendships, or even the challenges of growing up, praying for God's guidance is one of the best things you can do.

God cares about every part of your life, and He loves to be included in your thoughts, worries, and hopes.

Praying isn't about saying perfect words; it's about having an honest conversation with God. You could pray for wisdom, saying something like, "Lord, please help me make wise choices when it comes to my friends and the influences in my life."

Or, if you're feeling uncertain about a relationship, you could pray, "God, please show me if this friendship is one that brings me closer to You."

Simple prayers like these invite God to work in your life in amazing ways.

Asking God for guidance also helps you feel more peaceful when facing tough decisions.

If you're feeling uncertain or overwhelmed, take a moment to pray and ask God to help you see things clearly. He's always there, listening and ready to give you the wisdom you need.

You don't have to go through life alone, and God loves when you turn to Him for support. Growing up brings a lot of questions and choices, but praying for God's guidance helps you make those decisions with confidence. You'll find that when you invite Him into your life through prayer, you start seeing His hand in small and big ways.

God's guidance can come through a verse, a conversation with a friend or family member, or even a feeling of peace when you're uncertain.

Take your time building this habit. You might start with a short prayer each morning, thanking God for the day and asking Him to help you grow in wisdom.

Or, if you're facing a specific challenge, take a few moments to tell Him all about it and ask for His help.

Over time, you'll notice that praying becomes something you look forward to—a quiet time to share your heart with God.

As you continue this journey, remember that open communication, both with God and with trusted adults, creates a path of support, wisdom, and love that you can carry with you for the rest of your life.

Sharon L. Taylor

CHAPTER SEVEN

Embracing Your God-Given Identity Celebrating Our Unique Talents and Personalities

I remember feeling both curious and sometimes unsure about who I was.

Like you, I had things that made me excited, things that made me feel a little shy, and dreams that were all my own.

Part of growing up as a Christian is discovering that God created each of us with unique talents and personalities, and celebrating that uniqueness is part of honoring His design.

Think about some of the things you love to do.

Are you someone who enjoys drawing, singing, writing stories, or playing sports?

Maybe you're the friend who always knows how to make others laugh, or perhaps you're the one who's great at listening.

Each of these qualities is a special part of who God made you to be.

I truly believe that God gave each of us these talents and traits for a reason, and as we discover them, we also begin to see how we fit into His beautiful plan.

Celebrating our unique talents and personalities doesn't mean we're boasting or thinking we're better than others. It simply means recognizing that we're each a special piece of God's puzzle. When we embrace the way God made us, we can start to use our talents in ways that bless others and bring joy to ourselves.

For example, if you love helping others, maybe you can volunteer at your church or help out a neighbor.

If you're a great storyteller, perhaps you'll inspire others with stories that uplift and encourage them.

One way to explore your God-given talents is to try new things. Don't be afraid to explore different activities, classes, or hobbies. Sometimes we discover hidden talents by stepping out of our comfort zones.

Remember, even if you try something and realize it's not your thing, you've still learned something valuable about yourself. When you celebrate the unique ways God made you, you're also honoring His creativity.

After all, the Bible tells us in Psalm 139:14, "I praise you because I am fearfully and wonderfully made."

God designed every part of you with care and intention, and He delights in seeing you use your gifts. Take pride in who you are and remember that you have a unique role in this world—one that no one else can fill.

Understanding the Importance of Self-Love and Confidence

Self-love is a phrase we hear a lot these days, but what does it mean in a Christian context?

I like to think of self- love as seeing ourselves the way God sees us: as valuable, beloved, and worthy. God created each of us, and He doesn't make mistakes.

When we learn to love ourselves, we're also learning to honor God's work in us. Loving yourself doesn't mean you think you're perfect. None of us are!

But it does mean you can be kind to yourself, just as God is kind to you. Maybe you sometimes struggle with feeling "good enough" or worry about not measuring up.

If so, remember that God's love for you isn't based on being perfect. He loves you as you are, even with your imperfections. One way to practice self-love is by taking care of yourself.

This could mean eating healthy foods, getting enough sleep, and treating your body well. It also means filling your mind with positive thoughts. When you catch yourself thinking, "I'm not good at this," or "I'll never be like so-and-so," gently remind yourself that God doesn't compare you to anyone else.

He has a plan for you that's uniquely yours. Confidence comes naturally when we practice self-love.

Imagine that you're holding a treasure that's precious and irreplaceable—that treasure is you! When you understand your worth, you're able to step into the world with confidence, knowing you have something valuable to offer.

Confidence doesn't mean you won't ever feel nervous or doubt yourself; it means that, deep down, you know God has made you with purpose and love.

As you grow, you'll face moments when it's easy to doubt yourself. You might think, "I'm not good at this," or "Maybe I don't have what it takes."

During these times, go to God. Pray and ask Him to remind you of your value and your worth in His eyes. You'll find that the more you see yourself as God sees you, the easier it is to treat yourself with kindness and step forward with confidence.

Learning to Love Others as Christ Loves Us

Part of embracing your God-given identity means learning to love others the way Christ loves us. Jesus showed us that love is more than just feelings—it's about action, patience, and kindness.

As you grow, you'll meet people who are very different from you. They might look different, act differently, or even have different beliefs.

But as Christians, we're called to love others with the same grace and compassion Jesus showed. One of the most beautiful ways to reflect Christ's love is through kindness. Every time you help a friend, forgive someone, or go out of your way to make someone feel included, you're sharing the love of Jesus with the world.

Loving others doesn't mean you'll always agree with them, but it does mean you can treat them with respect and understanding.

There will be times when loving others is challenging. Maybe someone hurts your feelings or does something you disagree with. In moments like these, ask yourself, "How would Jesus want me to respond?" He teaches us to forgive, to seek peace, and to be humble.

By treating others with love, even when it's difficult, you become a reflection of Christ to those around you. Jesus also teaches us to love those who might be hard to love.

This doesn't mean you have to be best friends with everyone, but it does mean treating everyone with respect and kindness. When you show love in this way, you're not only honoring others, but you're also honoring God.

Building a Strong Relationship with God: Trust, Prayer, and Self-Worth

The most important relationship you'll ever have is the one you have with God. As you grow, you'll face challenges and choices, but having a strong relationship with God gives you a foundation to build on. When you trust God, pray to Him, and see yourself through His loving eyes, you gain a sense of self-worth that goes beyond what anyone else thinks of you.

Trusting God means knowing that He's with you, guiding you, and watching over you. There will be times in life when things feel uncertain or difficult, but remember that God has a plan for you.

Proverbs 3:5-6 encourages us to "Trust in the Lord with all your heart and lean not on your own understanding; in all your ways submit to him, and he will make your paths straight." This verse is a reminder that we don't have to figure everything out on our own—God is there to lead us.

Prayer is one of the best ways to build your relationship with God. You don't need fancy words or long prayers; just speak from your heart.

Tell God about your day, ask for His guidance, and thank Him for the blessings in your life.

As you make prayer a regular part of your life, you'll find that it brings you peace and comfort, even on difficult days. Understanding your self-worth in God's eyes is also a crucial part of building this relationship.

The world might try to tell you that your value is based on what you achieve or how you look, but God sees you differently.

Your worth comes from the fact that you are His child, made in His image and loved beyond measure.

Embracing this truth gives you the strength to face any challenge and the courage to be exactly who God created you to be. As you grow, remember that your identity isn't found in the opinions of others or the pressures of the world. Your true identity is found in Christ.

You are loved, valued, and made with purpose. Embracing your God-given identity allows you to live with joy, confidence, and a heart full of love for others.

Conclusion

Encouragement to Keep Growing in Faith and Understanding

As we come to the end of our journey together in this book, I want to remind you of something so important: this is just the beginning of a lifelong journey.

You've taken big steps to learn about God's plan for your body, your relationships, and your life, and I couldn't be prouder of you. Growing up is full of questions, choices, and sometimes even challenges, but God is with you every step of the way. He has a unique plan for you, and part of that plan is growing in faith, understanding, and love.

When I was your age, I often wondered if I'd ever truly understand all the things I was learning about God, faith, and myself.

Over time, I discovered that understanding isn't something we "arrive" at—it's something we build on little by little.

Each time you pray, read the Bible, or show love to someone, you're growing in your faith. God doesn't expect us to know everything right away, and He delights in walking with us as we discover more about Him and ourselves.

As you keep growing, you'll probably find that some topics feel confusing, and that's okay. It's perfectly normal to have questions, especially as you go through changes and face new experiences.

I encourage you to stay curious and keep asking those questions. Talk to your parents, a trusted adult, or a Christian mentor whenever you're unsure. Remember, God welcomes your questions, and He uses them to draw you closer to Him.

One of the most beautiful things about being a follower of Christ is that we're never alone. Not only do we have God guiding us, but we're also part of a larger family—the body of believers.

Surround yourself with friends and mentors who encourage you to keep growing in your faith. Seek out opportunities at church, join a youth group, or volunteer in ways that allow you to serve others.

Each time you step out in faith, you're not only learning about God, but you're also sharing His love with others. Sometimes, growth means stepping outside of our comfort zones.

Maybe there's an opportunity to help someone or stand up for what's right, even when it's hard. In these moments, remember that God equips you with courage and wisdom.

Trust that He's giving you everything you need to be brave and faithful.

A Prayer for Wisdom, Self-Control, and Kindness

One of my favorite ways to connect with God, especially during times of growth, is through prayer. I'd like to pray with you now as you continue on this path.

Think of this prayer as a moment to invite God to walk alongside you in every step you take, no matter how small or big. "Dear Heavenly Father, Thank you for loving us and for creating each of us with purpose, love, and care.

We're grateful for the amazing bodies, minds, and hearts you've given us. Thank you for guiding us through every stage of life and for teaching us about your plan for us.

Lord, I ask that you give us wisdom as we grow, so we can understand your teachings and make choices that honor you. Help us to be patient with ourselves when we feel unsure and to trust that you're leading us.

Fill us with a desire to know you more deeply and to seek you in all things.

Please give us self-control, Lord, so we can handle our emotions and reactions in ways that show kindness and respect. Help us to recognize when we need to pause, pray, and think carefully before we act.

Remind us that you're always there to help, especially when we feel overwhelmed.

Most of all, fill our hearts with kindness, so we can love others as you love us. Let our words, actions, and thoughts reflect your grace, compassion, and forgiveness. Teach us to see others through your eyes and to treat everyone with the love you have shown us. Thank you for the gift of growing in faith and understanding.

We're excited to continue learning and to live out your plan for us with joy and courage.

In Jesus' name, Amen." Prayer is one of the most powerful ways we can talk to God and seek His help. Never forget that you can turn to God anytime, whether you're feeling happy, sad, or anything in between.

He's always ready to listen, guide, and help you through anything you face.

Final Thoughts:

Moving Forward with Confidence in God's Love As we lose this book, I want to leave you with a message that's close to my heart: move forward with confidence in God's love. Growing up might feel overwhelming at times, but remember that you are never alone.

God created you with love, and His love is constant, unchanging, and deeper than anything we can fully understand.

One of the biggest lessons I've learned is that confidence doesn't come from having everything figured out or always being certain.

True confidence comes from knowing that God is by your side, guiding you every step of the way. It means trusting that even when things don't make sense, God has a plan. You can face any challenge, any change, and any question with courage because God has given you the strength and the wisdom to grow.

As you continue to grow in your faith, remember to celebrate who you are. God doesn't want you to be anyone else—He wants you to be you. Embrace your talents, your personality, and the things that make you unique.

Each of us has a role in God's kingdom, and He has a plan for your life that is just as meaningful and valuable as anyone else's. You're going to encounter people and experiences that shape who you are, and along the way, you might feel pressured to change or doubt your worth.

When that happens, take a moment to remember who made you. The same God who created the universe, the stars, and everything in between also created you. You are deeply loved, valued, and treasured by Him.

Keep surrounding yourself with people who encourage you to grow in faith.

Be open to learning, to asking questions, and to seeking God's guidance in everything you do. Remember, you're on a journey, and each step brings you closer to understanding God's love and plan for you.

And finally, remember that mistakes don't define you.

There will be times when you fall short or make decisions that you wish you hadn't.

When that happens, don't be too hard on yourself. God's grace is always there, offering forgiveness and a chance to start fresh. Learn from those moments, grow from them, and move forward knowing that God's love for you never changes.

I am so grateful for the opportunity to walk with you on this part of your journey. Thank you for being open, curious, and willing to learn about these important topics.

Laurie K. Thoma

Made in United States
Orlando, FL
12 May 2025

61241039R00052